Float

poems by

Wendy Miles

Finishing Line Press
Georgetown, Kentucky

Float

Copyright © 2022 by Wendy Miles
ISBN 979-8-88838-004-8 First Edition
All rights reserved under International and Pan-American Copyright Conventions.
No part of this book may be reproduced in any manner whatsoever without written permission from the publisher, except in the case of brief quotations embodied in critical articles and reviews.

Publisher: Leah Huete de Maines
Editor: Christen Kincaid
Cover Art: Anthony Ulinski
Author Photo: Anne Panning
Cover Design: Elizabeth Maines McCleavy

Order online: www.finishinglinepress.com
also available on amazon.com

Author inquiries and mail orders:
Finishing Line Press
P. O. Box 1626
Georgetown, Kentucky 40324
U. S. A.

Table of Contents

Gone 1

i. white bird, whirring

Float 5
On a Monday, What You May Have Known 6
Family Album: Scene from Box One 7
Self-Portrait Formed with Unrelated Contents 8
Egg 9
Pink Elephant 10
Distaff 11
And Your Childhood—What Was It Like? 12
Tether 13
They Have Not 14
Proximity 15
Divination, Sky 17
How Bad 18

ii. what else but circle

Those Who Once Lived There Return 21
The Song You Know 22
Self-Portrait with Magic and Swallowing 23
Memory, Virginia *or* When They Hear 24
An Idea of Home 26
The Thing Itself 27
Voice 28
Self-Portrait Fashioned from a Few Things I Will Never Be 29
Still Lives 30
Regarding the Redbud 31
The Green Place 32

iii. almost a happy room

Scrapbook: Scene from Page One 35
You Be the Poet 36
Some of the Birds 37
The Memories 38
Mezzo Morto 40
No Windows Blow Open: A Fairy Tale 41
How Far 42
The Postcard She Wanted to Get 43
Weeks Ago, Months Ago, Once 44
Tonight the Moon 45
This Too Is a Ceremony 46
My Brother and I Consider Our Father 47
Trees I Don't Know 48
The Water 49
Let Us Not Argue 50

For my mother, Helen

One need not be a chamber to be haunted

—Emily Dickinson

Gone

> *You are in your body*
> *like a plant is solid in the ground,*
> *yet you are wind.*
>   —Rumi

The skinny cat with one bad eye
sips from the birdbath again.

The apple tree greens its hard little fruits.
Burdens swarm around it in the grass.

He's gone now, your daughter says, and wind bends the leaves
  —that boy who tickled and pinched.

The cat's ridged tongue curls backward. You say,
  But wasn't he only a dream?

Dirt rings her ankles, bruises plumb-line her shins.
Her voice she passes like salt.

Inside beneath a painting of a horizon
oranges mold to the surface of a table.

Her voice is your child moving slowly through the yard.
Her voice as it agitates the burdens.

A tree at dusk is a reliquary.
There is so much sacred in a girl.

Inside the house, warm air presses
both sides of a small shut window.

A loose thread moves at the hem of your dress.
Sky closes the lid of a box.

i. white bird, whirring

Float

1.

An open door.
A child pauses on a step.
Her head turns, lifts to hear
her name float above the yard.
A child is an open door.

The child holds her breath
at the thought of what it means
—her name—stills
to hook it to herself with a bright pin.
A child is a breath.
A name is a bright pin.

2.

A low sink. An open window.
A mother leans at the low sink,
shirt off, breasts pressed to a towel.
Barely audible, *Oh,* she says, *it feels so good
you just can't believe it.*
A daughter is an open window, a folded towel.

Shampoo the scent of ginger.
Warm water pours from a plastic cup,
spreads along the mother's pink crown,
neck, around creases at the backs of ears.
The daughter breathes in the mother.
Water dribbles from the chin,
from the daughter's fingers.

A mother is a low sink, warm water.
Animal, *Animalis*: to have breath.
Love is a plastic cup. Love is a breath.

On a Monday, What You May Have Known

The dark hollow throat of a bird
        —caw-clack and pump of wings.

Mute tremor of the blue-tailed lizard
        —its slash across the white swing.

The sagging heads of marigolds
        bumped and bumped by the bee.

Or the trees, any of them, with their simple leaning,
lush ripple and heave in the wind.

If not trees, horses. One of them pulling
the quartered apple from your hand
        —its muzzle like corduroy.

When you back away, you glimpse the wing
ground into gravel, quills fanned and severed.

Separated from belly and beak, the wing is a name,
        an ache. You walk away

and you don't look back—the horse's coat like liquor,
        the apple gone to juice in its throat.

Family Album: Scene from Box One

Old Army tent, brother, me.
Matted grass, the stifling sour-green
mustiness we loved. The dog lingered, slapped
his beagle tail at the cloth wall. This is the moment
before the sunlight fell away, when the canvas flap
left one sharp seam of light—
brother, me, crouched inside.

Self-Portrait Formed with Unrelated Contents

Don't look at the girl pirouetting over the cattle guard even if
she's wearing a pink gingham bikini in the evening. This isn't
about nightshade plants or sinewy cats floating the fence line.
We have other fish to fry after the migraine aura leaves her limbs
and lips numb as a stroke. Okay, the cattle guard is true. And there was
an orange elephant bank, petunias in pots, and a little row to hoe.
But listen. There was mercy. She came to god and her days
cracked apart like jackhammered cement and the stairs wobbled
and the mother said she was brand new and the girl in gingham—it's true—
went on about her business. Her business was watching out
for the sky to be right. Listening for a car door in the dark. Twisting
banana ice pops in her mouth and not dangling her clean bare legs
in places where she knew good and well snakes could be.

Egg

Make an arc of your hand. Move the egg from nest
to basket. The henhouse door sags. Note the cardinal,
bees, rusted nail, the gate. Straw swims in the cuff
of your jeans. Beetles cloud peonies, a black snake
coils on a rock. One warm egg is slick with blood.

Down the road city girls wait in the big gold house
lilting *ma'am* and *please* until you're alone on the porch.
One finger to your collarbone, they ask if you know how to swim.
Their mother wears perfume, slathers lotion, pats your knees.
They dive for coins, your shoulders above the surface as they kick.

Once, at an egg hunt, a girl ate raw peas. Pop on her tongue.
Candy skins gleamed in the grass, on church steps, on bricks
below a silver oil tank. Your basket knocked along. *Up*
your mother said. *Up* to the crook of the tree, to the gold
goose egg. And the other girl, pop. Flutter of jacket as she ran.

Pink Elephant

The animal sat on its haunches on my dresser,
front legs lifted as if it were a dog, begging,
and the trunk curled cheerily—the whole unit
doubling as hair dryer with vinyl bonnet or nightlight.

So as I retched, vomit in strings down the inside
of my pink trashcan, my mother's hand flat
on my back, we were both enclosed in that light.
She would raise my arms, slip off the wet nightgown,

rub a warm washcloth all around my neck,
the ribs, my back, up and down both shoulders,
ending with the wrists. Then a dry, fresh gown
and the covers returned. I could watch

my mother gather the limp fabric, the rag,
the can, and see the elephant's taut cheeks blush.
One window of my room faced the back of the house
where the cat I loved slept. I'd crawl out,

haul her in and hoist myself back over
the brick ledge. Sometimes I'd sit her on the dresser,
put the elephant bonnet on her head.
The next morning, swollen eyes, crusted lashes.

Allergies were confirmed, but my mother
did not take them away—the cats picking through
the long night grass, their serenade of soft mewling
drifting to me through the screen.

Distaff

Standing in her thick robe she breathed his scent—whiskey, cured ham,
the cold. It was Christmas Eve, my brother and I small. Our mother
had appeared to help set out Santa Claus for us—a used and complicated
bowling set, a doll named my name in a dark blue dress. At our general store,
it had been a week of raffles and turkey shoots. My brother had cut out
circles of poster board to set spinning on the nail outside, men and boys
ready in coveralls to judge the spray of holes one bullet left. Our mother
had sliced bacon, hoop cheese, weighed and wrapped it, her handwritten
price like a spray of ivy.

He sent her back to bed, set the few toys out himself, saying to enjoy it now
—when we got older, she could do it herself. At his parents' house
the next day, my aunts—hair pulled tight in red yarn—clapped as we
showed them our presents. In turtlenecks, new underwear, socks
our mother had chosen, my brother and I placed our toys—one each—
on the floor at our father's feet. From the short car ride they were icy
in our hands. Then—called to the kitchen—our mother disappeared.

And Your Childhood—What Was It Like?

I can tell you in dogs—the brown-and-white beagle,
tumor at the neck, the one who buried my new pants

near the watermelons that never ripened.
In jars of canned tomatoes (the steam and grip).

In the old gold truck, my father's coveralls, guns,
harmonicas strewn on the dash.

(The metal-and-tractor-grease smell.) I can tell you
in green, in dirt, in clods of red clay, a rusted aqua swing

that sliced my inner calf. In potatoes—the white quartz rocks
I piled into pyramids at the end of tilled patches

—the seed spreader (its industry and ease). In corn.
My brother's shirts, each sleeve cut to cover an arm

(to reach the ropy pods and twist,
the milky-sweet smell that clung).

In grass, in hay, and the green kitchen stove,
the big bed angled in the front room—theirs—

(if you stepped through the door).
I can tell you in weariness.

In black cattle plodding (dust motes rising).
In the gust of a train, its detonating blare.

And snow—once with a deep sheen of ice
I walked across, my father setting off

to open the store. It was *bread and gas,*
and *I'll stay if I have to.* My mother silent, watching.

Tether

Balanced in a scrap of weedy grass—
pink streamers and the white banana seat
seem to be a complicated grief.

The bike isn't mangled. Pale ribbons
nest in its handlebars like belief:
the child will return to her life,

wander home older but undamaged,
gently collapse her body—long-limbed—
to the slight frame. Whirl of wheel, grind of chain.

Her still-luminous long blonde hair . . . will fly.

~

Her still-luminous long blonde hair will fly

to the slight frame. Whirl of wheel, grind of chain.
Gently collapse her body—long-limbed.
Wander home older but undamaged.

The child will return to her life,
nest in its handlebars like belief:
the bike isn't mangled. Pale ribbons

seem to be a complicated grief.
Pink streamers and the white banana seat
balance in a scrap of weedy grass.

They Have Not

—after Sally Mann

These girls. They have not endured
between their legs—not yet—the slick hot
wet of blood. No pinch has come
to thrumming ovary.

No swell. No loss. By now
they have only their own supple
skins encasing easy
flawless bones.

These two, the perfect birds
of their small feet nested
in the cool tickle of grass, feel
only sunlit heat.

This summer's dust has sheathed for them
one bitter blade of womanhood: child-
birth. Those far-off days—for now—are
boxed, tagged.

One day that hip won't jut
into the same angle, the blonde
at each forehead may darken, pearly nipples
may drench in milk.

But this moment—really—is as far
as we can go: the candy cigarette, one
doll clutched, the way we want
to know, know

from those eyes where, from these girls
how far.

Proximity

1.

When the woman's husband took sick
the dog showed up in her backyard.
It gulped old butter beans dumped
in the field at the corner of the fence.

Visitors filled the house, but the beagle
shied from touch. She got biscuits, ham,
slept in the ditch across the road. A bowl
was filled with water, weighted with a rock.

Dry dog food was sprinkled in the grass.
When the woman walked to the mailbox
she listened for the claw-tick on the road,
felt that living thing's breath at her heels.

2.

The teenage girl down the street
lingers near a boy, his polished car
parked quickly, in the wrong direction.
He leans forward, thrums the steering wheel,

door flung into her parents' light-heaped yard.
Music floats between them. The muffled bass
kicks. She bends one arm, holds an elbow
from behind her back. He's inches from the curb.

Birds peck through the grass near the house.
He's one step from her lean arms, tanned legs.
Her toes curl the rough curb while her soles
—creamy—flash like halves of the moon.

3.

They're gone now, the old couple. Him,
Parkinson's. Her, a fallen bladder, a split knee.
The neighbor took up mowing. He weeded
around the stoop and the silent white urns.

The geraniums went stemmy, stained
red wherever petals fell. In the newspaper
there's a picture—a woman who disappeared
thirty years ago. Her eyes will always be green.

When the weathered birdhouse fell
it didn't crack apart but lay on its side.
The neighbor lifted it, leaving a mark
where it had been like a wound undressed.

4.

Every year it was the smell of cedar.
The black cat, back arched in screech
on the picture-window. The pumpkin-man,
elbows pinned to the front door, hands limp.

Until October all the dark paper things
that opened into tissue pumpkins or moons
lined the chest in my mother's room. Once,
I returned a scarecrow, its body halved like wings,

and I saw my parents' letters bundled with string.
I pinched one loose, slipped it under my shirt.
Then the red-jet airmail stamp, my mother's name,
the empty pocket I found beneath an already cut seam.

Divination, Sky

A spool of smoke unwinds across the sky.
Crow clack, cicada, bodies open to the sky.

In 79 AD ash and roasting heat seal an envelope
around Herculaneum; they look but find no sky.

But the heart remains. See it telescope the chest,
long for the moon's pull, that flight to the sky.

Cyrano knew it—the little magnet in the boat
rocking, hands around the ball, heave of the sky.

Archaeologists excavate a woman: gold bracelets,
divination of pelvis, childless, arms closed to the sky.

I know her. Bracelets tinkle, soles scald on ash.
Her Vesuvius—black cauldron dumping the sky.

In a room I dream—a painting of a little blue boat.
Outside the yard is bristled weed, busted rock, sky.

How Bad

Again and again my mother's hands rubbed her eyes.
She said I'd rather die than this. Her womb's blood
an unbuttoned fever, her hands that pushed me away.

Once I fell on a nail. Hanging in my chin it grazed teeth.
My mother wiggled it out, said Yes, yes honey,
you know anything that bleeds this much will hurt.

When they brought me home a newborn
I mottled in car-window sun. My father
shook his head: A girl. This delicate girl.

I was nine when my blood came to me.
Clockworks ticked, my body-mechanism
lodged in its pawls. I opened. I reached up,

kissed my father goodnight, the way they did on TV
—mouth closed, a movie-star twisting my face over his—
and, from his disgust, learned then how bad I could be.

ii. what else but circle

Those Who Once Lived There Return

There where a golden bird is made
golden by October's slanting light,

through the threshold of the hidden house
the empty clothes are seated in chairs.

The threshold gone, go ahead
and float. No one to see. Listen.

One loose shingle shifts
and forever tumbles.

A wooden drawer wails,
one hammer hitched on scissors.

You know something lies dead
across the road. Barbed wire fence,

rusted, looks to have uprooted posts
and embedded itself in tight periphery.

Even so, how can anyone sleep
with the windows nailed shut?

Can the bird know how golden
its body becomes? If you place the cup,

twist the dishrag, fold it in such a way,
look out the window again. You saw once

a cat snatched up by a hawk, legs
splayed straight as sticks.

How those bodies merged.
How those bodies merged

and awakened the air.

The Song You Know

      Thunder across the clean hayfield
hard crack of dirt on the metal gate

      —the yard—
and everything else

      Your father's white undershirt
folded along his ribs, yellowed under the arms

      kitchen light and pan-clack
saccharine apple trees

bees in the tube of the ear
the song you know, rain

on the way—a hovering—
      the stick of thick grass

      arches pricked flat
to the clover, you run

      brother behind, his breath
      wind. While your father

loops wire—that knock
of latch to rusted metal.

      What couldn't find its way in?

Self-Portrait with Magic and Swallowing

At times it was like this, wasn't it. Barn after rickety barn
and a series of cloudy directions. Sometimes night
curled in your fleshy young mouth. There's no cure
for the dark birds you've eaten. Through the tall grass
a beautiful couple comes swaggering into view.
They've been ambling with the water dogs again.
Yes, there's a house here hidden from view.
Yes, the deer bed in that thicket.
Two leisurely bodies ease one into another
like rope coiling over itself. The smell of water,
bailing twine, honeysuckle, dusk. Yes,
someone is dying. Blood slogs through the body
and flesh tugs at flesh. Copper-penny taste on the tongue.
There's the tuneful splash of water bird or dog.
Delicate bones collect—each churned out clean from your lips.

Memory, Virginia *or* When They Hear

1.
At the cemetery
flowers are feathers
pulled along a palm.

2.
The wife sits, outlandish,
in a fluorescent room.
Wet boots inside a plastic bag.

St. Mary's Hospital,
sky so white it dizzies.
There is the husband.

They winch up his stomach,
stitch pink remains.
The tumor had thickened and clung.

Now snow
and snow
and snow.

3.
Clammy lamplight.
Cross-legged in pajamas, paper plates
nest in the children's laps.

The wife's voice,
Spread this paper towel across your knees.
Snow falls.

The husband's voice,
She told you once. Braided rug beneath them.
Curtains puffed with heat.

Everything already somehow known
when they hear
the soft loft of bird-sound

falling,
falling
through the cool dark.

They put down their plates, their talk.
The porch light thumps on.
They see

in the dark arms of the pecan tree
a white owl—
its face a small moon.

They do not speak but only look.
Then the wife. *Come back*, she says
meaning *inside*.

The bird turns to them
and the moon-faced thing
—its small heart whirring—

will not be called a ghost for many years.

An Idea of Home

That was years ago, the old cat my mother didn't trust
that loped along the fencerow, circling in on the idea of home—
belly a jostling swag of kittens. I don't know how much time passed

before my mother gave up saying, Wendell, I know
you took that cat off once, but it wasn't far enough.
Twice. Three times. So many miles. But the cat walked home,

had the kittens under the silver oil tank. My father laughed
and called her *fine old girl, a good mama.* And I learned patience.
I was five. I named her Fat Cat. She made sure her babies had enough.

I'd seen them slide out—each purple-red body. And in our silence
I learned about mothers. One day I stretched my arm too far
through the white plank fence and she scratched me—deep. Her impatience

with me drew blood. The hay waggled and shined. In that spring air
at the edge of the field that curled around our yard—this time
my mother holding me, my tears rivering her arms—we saw how far

that mama cat would go. We heard the snake crunch, saw it glimmer like flame
from the cat's mouth. Encircling the three of us—all that green, all that time.

The Thing Itself

They listen for the click
of the bed down the hall, the choke-spit
of the oxygen tank.

His pills dropping
onto a plate, the clean ping
of him still living. What they don't hear
—neither wife nor daughter—
is the thing itself.

But they taste it, smeared
across teeth, hunched
in their throats.

So they listen. If they hear
a rare cough rip, skitter through the sunlit room,
they almost hope.

                When it finally comes, they are surprised

that the house fills with sweetness, that they see
a doe grazing in a slant of lamplight,
a white possum shambling over birdseed in the moonlit grass,
eating as the feeder rocks above.

Voice

At sunset I head to my brother's farm.
Now bright new yellow lines divide the road.
All these years we've driven it without harm,
sure there wasn't one curve we didn't know.
But still the same fields. They loll and usher
hay and walnut through my open windows.
The sun this warm September evening flushes
the still-green leaves, spreads yellow across the road.

He walks fencerows, calls to his cows
with a border collie who splays and rolls
if you say *bang*. Almost two years since our
father died. At the barn my brother's voice
climbs through the dusk as swallows dip, then rise.
    I linger for that sound against the sky.

Self-Portrait Fashioned from a Few Things I Will Never Be

peanut queen with a festival gown

peanuts stitched with fishing line to lace

soaked guy who says *weather's part of the party*

boy set aglow palming fresh basketball

lush perfume held in rain-beaded peony

daughter who ruins father's meal with perfume

inside a painting of a little blue boat

inside a painting called *house near horizon*

festive dress rumpled in dark steamer trunk

the question *what if the horizon were without the old house?*

person who doesn't take it personally

or current resident typed below her name

needles pushed through papery husks

only witness to moths fluttering up from the trunk

the question *what if you're making this sadder than it is?*

the question *how could a gown disintegrate in flight?*

the wings, the dust, and a little blue boat

Still Lives

1.

The sky sits close to the window and rocks
its broad blue, its one smear of cloud. Thanksgiving
narrates with timer, ice-clink, table leaves lifting.

The hunters' talk is muted. It drapes the driveway.
Against a truck's tailgate, the soft knock and scrape
of a still-warm body limp on the rippled steel.

2.

Her unrelenting heart astounds us. For three years
our grandmother lay immobile—legs purpling,
bowels and kidneys loose, the soft meat of her sinking in.

On the last day her heart forces breaths at seven per minute.
A plastic sunflower bobs at her window like a child's noggin.
She's told you how much it has grown.

3.

On the second-floor ceiling, a pattern swirled
by Virginia creeper, the pin-dot stencil its echo. Children's
mildewed shoes curled on their sides. Busted windows.

Of course a Blue Horse notebook left blank. The tin roof silver
after seventy years. But what of the clean-swept room?
The inky-eyed blooms of pawpaw closing in?

Regarding the Redbud

The redbud by the fence will have to come out.
The stump will have to be ground down.

There were no caterpillar sacks strewn through limbs.
No storm glued icy branches to the frozen earth.

A friend tells me a cardinal loops her maple,
hits her back window, drops, ascends.

Twelve times the animal has done this. Maybe
it wants to die. My father did, toward the end.

Through the phone, the expert's voice is deep.
He says, regarding the redbud: *canker.*

It started in the trunk, spread slowly.
I don't ask him this: What could help but die?

From the window I see the birdfeeder empty, sway.
No use longing for flutter or song.

The Green Place

—after Jon Anderson

Day filters through to evening.
First the cedars, their green,
then copper patinas the field
—every high thing letting down toward night.

Swallows tangle redbud, leaving
thin cracks in the sky to be filled again
by dusk. And the trees yield
to the hush, the barest pink light

of a clear winter day nudged to evening.
Bright berry of holly, the blackening
barn and the farthest tree-lined field
back away behind the night.

All the warmth closes out, leaves
a cold bell of red clay to thud again
beneath the pasture, make it yield
to hollow blue-black until tomorrow, until the light.

iii. almost a happy room

Scrapbook: Scene from Page One

My mother's only scrapbook holds a crushed corsage.
There's always a crushed corsage—its long pearl pin still in.
It sprawls like an animal in decay, bruised yellows
and blues pulling loose.

You Be the Poet

Her two hands hold the gift for you—a fluttering plume
at her back: wings. Tiny Eros bearing the golden quiver.
Why can't she be a god, this girl?

Make her the god. Why can't she hold the secret of love,
seize it—dark dove—and cage it in her chest? Why can't she
parcel out her love in cotton? So light it has to be glued down.

It makes sense. And if you want it to be, it will.
And will you be Chaos, out of whom she, your sex,
this little god, becomes? Okay then. Make her real.

Make her quick, clever, and whatever happens next, please
do this much: make the red paper prick your cheek.
Try this: make the story never end. Make her hands

deliver the strange-familiar feeling of becoming. Make the day
a mysterious spectacle. Make her hair dark, ambiguous.
When she hands you the cotton, paper, glue, and you,

a father, a man, stand there in the air you invented
and get that feeling that is, for now, nameless . . . take a minute.
Figure out what to do next. Try to make her hands delicate

yet strong. Try to convey gratitude, yet dread that somehow,
no matter what you do—in that moment between your touch
and her turning, calling over her shoulder, gone already—

what comes next won't be enough. But get used to it
—all this—because from now on, realize, that's how it is.

Some of the Birds

At first it's difficult to understand. At first
he asks you questions he thinks are simple.

Why would a bird fly slowly? Acid lolls
on his tongue. *It's no good,* he says.

I'm doused in nightshade and I ache all night—
knuckles and bunions burning.

He tells you *I'm of three minds. Like these damn birds.
Coffee's no good either.*

He won't let you turn down the bed, hang
the new calendar he got from the bank,

set the big digital clock, or see about the imaginary cat
—sick for days, curled in his laundry, reeking of piss.

You don't have to understand. From the med cart
in the hall you see him skulk through blue television light.

You tell yourself this could be worse.
He bends. His room goes golden. He faces you.

You know, he says, *it's the beginning of the solution
when the thunder is under the lake.*

His arms begin to lift. You have kids at home.
Ten-for-ten frozen beef entrees. A cracked toilet.

When you get home your husband will be asleep.
You'll shower and drink a cup of tea. You start toward him.

In a voice not rimmed in ruin, he half-sings,
Some of the birds fly slowly. There is no reason why.

The Memories

The memories took it hard that year,
all the stars gleaming like that.
And the photographs—another insult.

Dolls tugged by armload from the basement.
The road to the dump riddled with potholes,
plastic arms pointing from the truck cab.

The memories just fingered their nylon hair,
pushed them in strollers, wheels whistling.

Abandoned memories clung to the window.
There was the father. There was the mother,
face streaked behind a roof of hands.

Anyone could have mistaken those memories
for rain the way they wept.

Old memories curled in the neck of a sweater and—
nostalgic, spinning the wheel of the toy motorcycle—
gazed at the steady light of the Easy-Bake oven.

One anxious memory scraped her back
slipping under the fence. There was
the loose, rusted nail. There was the mother.

Plump pinch of wasp and gasoline heat
to the bone. A wet cigar—sopping tobacco
drew out the sting. She asked

*Who would you want to live with,
me or him? I'm just asking you—who?*

It's thankless being a memory.

One Sunday-memory skulked
toward the old pink bedroom, slumped
on the bed, ran a hand across the spread.

After awhile the room might have been
almost a happy room. Her skinny legs.
Corduroys that matched her shirt.

There was her heartbeat thumping. There too
was the wood-grain wolf revealing itself
in the hollow veneer door across the hall.

So there was the eddy in the gut.
There was the darkness entering.

There were the stars being eaten.
There were the old cows lumbering.
There were the cats set with night vision.

There was the weight of a hand
light as—lighter than—a doll's.

Mezzo Morto

Driving that evening three years prior
I trailed an idle contour of taillights.
The radio plunked. And from the safety
of a steep embankment a deer—
one white doe—edged near the road.

I couldn't have known that I would wait
with my mother at night, stare out a window,
both of us regulated to the medicine times.

Lortab, Phenergan—so many he made his own lists.
His Xanax and then—every ten minutes—
the morphine. No, we couldn't have expected
our need to stop his pain, even when there was
no more breath, not any sound.

His pulse lingered minutes
under my mother's hands.
She held him, watched him breathe
    —thought she watched—that pull of air,
the rise of chest, before I climbed,
    finally, over the sink to slide
behind them in the still-damp shower,
    take over the body for her.

No Windows Blow Open: A Fairy Tale

In the dream looms a boy I once kissed.
Me, a girl pleading for mouth aflame.
But from the alcove no birds launch. No windows
blow open, no leaves skitter through dust,
an unlocked door was never locked,
any chase has stopped.

Something—not grease—gums the kitchen floor
and a painting of a little blue boat
becomes a place a girl knows not to go.
Stairs twist to attic, the wall's sheen
bathes hatchet, its grip, the descent.
Through bristled weed, busted rock: a door.

Another house. White gingerbread slants,
interior lit red, men not-quite sleeping.

How Far

1.

One photo of my mother:
coal-black hair, red-red lipstick
she's not worn since, baby-doll pajamas,
tanned legs bent at the knees, slack
floral bedspread sprawled beneath her.

2.

A Halloween party:
peeled grapes for eyeballs.
My eyes covered, fingers skimming.
They rock loosely on a metal tray
       —in my mind bright-bloody, socketless.
A man's voice guides me through a room,
hand on my shoulder, hand at my back.

3.

Cherry-stem tying:
His eager, turned-on face.
The way he watches, has a stake,
desires every part of her mouth.
The stiff knot on the tongue
       —the prize cooling in the air.
Its taste already slipping down the throat.

The Postcard She Wanted to Get

Baby,
Tonight there's only this little green room
to tell you about. It's bleak. If you were here
the lamplight across the bed would look like September,
that black hair of yours spread out. I hear
there's a decent fish place down the road.
And good music a few blocks up. Couple of fellows
are headed out. But everything's kind of dry
and one-note without you. I know I told you
I don't need this hassle. But if I could cup
your face in my hands, put my mouth over yours,
I'd erase it all, breathe it back. Never happened.
See, without you it goes mostly like this:
wall, window, hour.

Weeks Ago, Months Ago, Once

My father came home once
late on a fourth of July to find the house
already dark. He didn't want a tepid supper
on a plate in a dark house, not even his own.
He stayed outside, lit one Roman candle,
dodged the fuse to look up—jaws slack—
at the white-hot sparks through black.
Even then the course seemed set:
his small contentments fleeting, sent skyward.

Months ago my father dreamed
catastrophe: His truck lost brakes,
lugged heavy into our driveway.
Another truck, headed toward its delivery,
paused to ignite in flame while my father
—limp—sat in the passenger seat
of his own truck—soundless—
as the delivery truck fell away, lost
down an embankment, flames stroking
frantic sunlit air but where
there was no truck for the finding,
only grass, air, a circle of flame.

Out in his yard just weeks ago
my father walked round and round
its wide perimeter, talking to a boyhood friend,
the two of them receding, receding
in a feeble arc into the west, reemerging
from the east at the lip of the driveway.
                              By then,

we understood the multiplying cells
in his sternum, knew the churn, the ache,
imagined the gray fist of tumor opening
its too-strong hand, spreading flat its wet,
long fingers, each white knuckle—as it pulled closed—
a ratchet fitting into every secret pawl my father held,
circling. Circling. What else but circle?

Tonight the Moon

Tonight the moon shakes loose through the house.

The kitchen—little table, folding chairs—
holds the long-baked tang of sweet potatoes.

No need to check. The back door's bolted.

It has been for days. The yellow rocker faces
the cracked garden. It lists forward, back.

Peppers used to swell, tomatoes bowed their vines.

She can't remember everything. But once this house
was theirs. In the front room he slept, buttoned

to her grandmother—a woman afraid of everything.

From the doorway she sees the gold-bottomed lamp
is missing. The orange ceramic horse. And the bed

where once each delicate foot bone was sheltered.

This Too Is a Ceremony

—after a NOVA *episode on the Lucky Leakeys,* "Becoming Human"

Don't tell the archaeologist not to look for a heart.
One brush may unearth it, tapered finger of one hand.

There is talk of Lake Turkana; its undulating silted bed
may hold the creation of compassion, which must be hands.

Mercy may rest in a jawbone, its ancient abscess a bed
of evidence; survival without teeth means help from other hands.

The digging we know can return us to ourselves, deliver hearts,
or parts the heart touched—pelvis, eye socket, slim tibia, hand.

We exalt these traces. Exultation is a ceremony of the heart.
We place in order the objects of our praise, align them with hands.

Evidence loves the finding. See the light O'Keefe's hands
brought to Stieglitz. Each offered tendon more feather than hand.

Dying unheld—this too is a ceremony, that absence, cool bed.
My name detached, someone will lift the body with her own two hands.

My Brother and I Consider Our Father

I was of three minds
—Wallace Stevens

Moving slowly over the shadowed fields
every white cloud billows and seems to yield
mostly to the birds, but also to us.
One brother, one sister, who lift our eyes,
recognize the crows, their vacant peels.

You've driven our father's old GMC
—that dilapidated whistle of steel,
vehicle for harmonicas and dust.
In the whirring body of a bird days spool.

Realms of unknowing will not be revealed.
Ghost—father—on a tractor, rakes the field
in the heat of July and won't discuss
not canning snaps and all those tomatoes.
It's cold now, but there are things we can't feel.
And in the body of a bird time spools.

Trees I Don't Know

—for my father, Wendell

You were the one who walked the fencerows,
told me the names. Crabapple, its heavy red swags.
Chestnut, Sycamore, the tall Pawpaw with its black
blooms looming. I was the one who only listened.

Lately I've seen trees I don't know. Without you
I've learned one is Osage-orange, green fruit balls
bigger than walnuts, rutted like brains that fall apart
under tires along an old driveway twenty miles from home.

I gave you a squirrel-proof feeder. That was for the cancer
two brittle Decembers ago. But the chain at the heart
of the limb was too high. And you thought the squirrel was too smart.
You scratched through your tool room, found a leash never used.

You worked to loop it over a branch but couldn't
anymore lift a ladder. So you cranked your truck,
steered backward through the yard, and with the back cab window,
knocked seed to the bed of the truck. For the smallest birds

you lifted your body to the tailgate and to the Willow Oak you planted
nearly forty years before. Behind you Kudzu haunted the power line
along the road and the fields where cows plodded toward
your voice every evening. The tall Oak was there, the Hickory.

From the porch I saw the loose work shirt, your dark brown hat.
Breath held, I waited for you to come back down.

The Water

The ghosts were there. Shale green walls
so cool. Floating at the tip of the stairs.

Latches all over clicked and clicked.
It was always the same.

Coming upon it
through the last cluster of trees.

Anytime someone you love leaves a room
and you wish they wouldn't.

I placed my faith in the road
that led to the water.

Each of us leaves a suggestion.
It was the road and coming upon the water.

Was it a house or a premonition.
People flocked the far bank.

No one walks to the water alone.
There are ghosts. There are clusters of trees.

Let Us Not Argue

Let us not argue.

Living, we are restless. We get ahead of ourselves. Grief enters

like a bad houseguest and before we know it he's pushing us around,

singing off key, dragging out old photos and putting them back all wrong.

Take heart.

There where a golden bird was once made golden by October's slanting light

those who once lived there return—empty clothes wondrously seated in chairs.

There is the mother who pats out biscuits, puts them with sliced plump tomato

and fresh fried apple.

There are the donkeys that nuzzle at the barbed wire fence.

There is the long expanse of hay bales stretched over the farthest knoll.

There is the deer who comes to the fence and brings his doe.

There is the stray dog who eats from an old pie pan weighted with a rock.

There are the children gluing model airplanes and waiting in doorways.

There is the one willow oak that buckles the sidewalk.

The day it was planted there was only the future—one horizon blue and green.

It is evening now.

If grief is a guest, eventually he will head off to bed in another room,

having said too much.

Let us not argue.

Whoever we are, memory swings up inside our throats.

Let us be kind.

Our dead. Who is to say how much we love them.

Acknowledgments

I offer grateful acknowledgement to the editors of the following publications in which various poems in this book first appeared—sometimes in different form.

Alabama Literary Review: "On a Monday, What You May Have Known" and "And Your Childhood—What Was It Like?" and "The Memories"
2012 *Anthology of Appalachian Writers, Volume IV*: "Trees I Don't Know"
Burningword Literary Journal: "Self-Portrait Formed with Unrelated Contents" and "Self-Portrait with Magic and Swallowing"
Caesura: "Voice"
The Comstock Review: "You Be the Poet"
The Dos Passos Review: "Family Album: Scene from Box One" (published as "Family Album: Scenes from Boxes One and Two") and "*Mezzo Morto*"
Flock: "Gone"
Hunger Mountain: "Divination, Sky"
Image/Word: a book of poems: "They Have Not"
The MacGuffin: "This Too Is a Ceremony"
Palette Poetry: "The Water"
The Pedestal Magazine: "Still Lives"
Prairie Schooner: "Self-Portrait Fashioned from a Few Things I Will Never Be" and "The Song You Know"
R.kv.r.y Quarterly Literary Journal: "Those Who Once Lived There Return"
Richmond Magazine: "Egg"
Southern Poetry Review: "The Thing Itself"
storySouth: "Proximity"
Tupelo Quarterly: "The Postcard She Wanted to Get"
Voices from the Attic: "Float"
Yalobusha Review: "Regarding the Redbud"

Many thanks to Monica Dalton who knew the whole time; Anne Panning and June Spence who have shared the pain and sheltered me; Sarah Jane Brubaker who always, always showed up; Marilyn Bousquin who helped me get angry; Steve Dawson who loved "Egg"; Mara Amster who said all the right things; Bunny Goodjohn who gave manuscript suggestions; Carrington Connelly—a spirit guide; Judie Connelly who funded a writing retreat in a villa; Nicole Smith Boyd—my adopted sister; Theresa Torisky and Michelle Gil-Montero who brought me to St. Vincent's; Donald Platt and Loren Graham who were my college teachers; Virginia Center for the Creative Arts residencies and fellow residents; Bowling Green State University's MFA program; Randolph College and University of Lynchburg; Joan Houlihan who advised me at a Colrain Poetry Manuscript Conference; James River Writers for their Best Poetry Contest and Joshua Poteat who selected my poem "Egg" as the winner in 2012; Carlow University and Madwomen in the Attic; Yona Harvey who chose the poem "Float" for the 2014 Patricia Dobler Poetry Award; Jan Beatty who made me sound great in a radio interview; Ilya Kaminsky and Dorianne Laux for recognizing my work; Stephen Dunn and David St. John—my cherished teachers who made it feel possible; Gary Short who accompanied me through the tsunamis; Allison Wilkins (Home Skillet), Jon Pineda and Sarah Freligh who graciously blurbed this book; Anthony Ulinski for the gorgeous cover art; Finishing Line Press for the opportunity; all the editors of publications in which my individual poems have been published; all my other friends, colleagues and former students who supported and encouraged me; Helen Miles, my mother, who said things like, "Now that's a good one."

Wendy Miles has published her work in places such as *Prairie Schooner, Tupelo Quarterly, The Chattahoochee Review, Southern Poetry Review* and *Hunger Mountain*. Yona Harvey selected her poem "Float" as the winner of the 2014 Patricia Dobler Poetry Award. Wendy holds an MFA in creative writing from Bowling Green State University and lives in Lynchburg, VA, with her dog Sugi. She is currently at work on another poetry collection titled *Plump for Prey*.

www.ingramcontent.com/pod-product-compliance
Lightning Source LLC
Chambersburg PA
CBHW030226170426
43194CB00007BA/872